GARDEN

PUBLISHING CO.

www.gardenpublishingco.com

ISBN 978-1-7355464-0-7
Cover design by Whitney Whitt
Illustrated by Whitney Whitt.
Printed in the United States of America.

HOLY SPIRIT
AND ME

Written by Jessica Doggett

Illustrated by Whitney Whitt

HOLY SPIRIT

is like the ocean waves. His presence gently washes
over me and pulls me closer to Him.

HOLY SPIRIT

is like a friend who whispers in your ear. He tells me the sweetest stories about the Father.

HOLY SPIRIT

is like the electricity in a light bulb. He gives me the power to do what Jesus did, and even greater things.

HOLY SPIRIT

is like decoding a secret message. He gives me the ability to understand heavenly messages.

HOLY SPIRIT

is like having a cup phone conversation. He speaks to me, and I can share what He tells me with everyone.

HOLY SPIRIT

is like being tickled by my daddy. He brings me joyful
laughter that makes me happy.

HOLY SPIRIT

is like a blanket fort. He keeps me protected, and
meets with me there in secret.

I Pledge

HOLY SPIRIT

is like saying the Pledge of Allegiance. With my words and actions I stand and honor Him.

HOLY SPIRIT

is like riding a giant roller coaster! He is so full of joy, mysteries and excitement.

HOLY SPIRIT

is like a mommy gently removing a Band-Aid from
a cut. He restores and heals the hurting places with
one gentle touch.

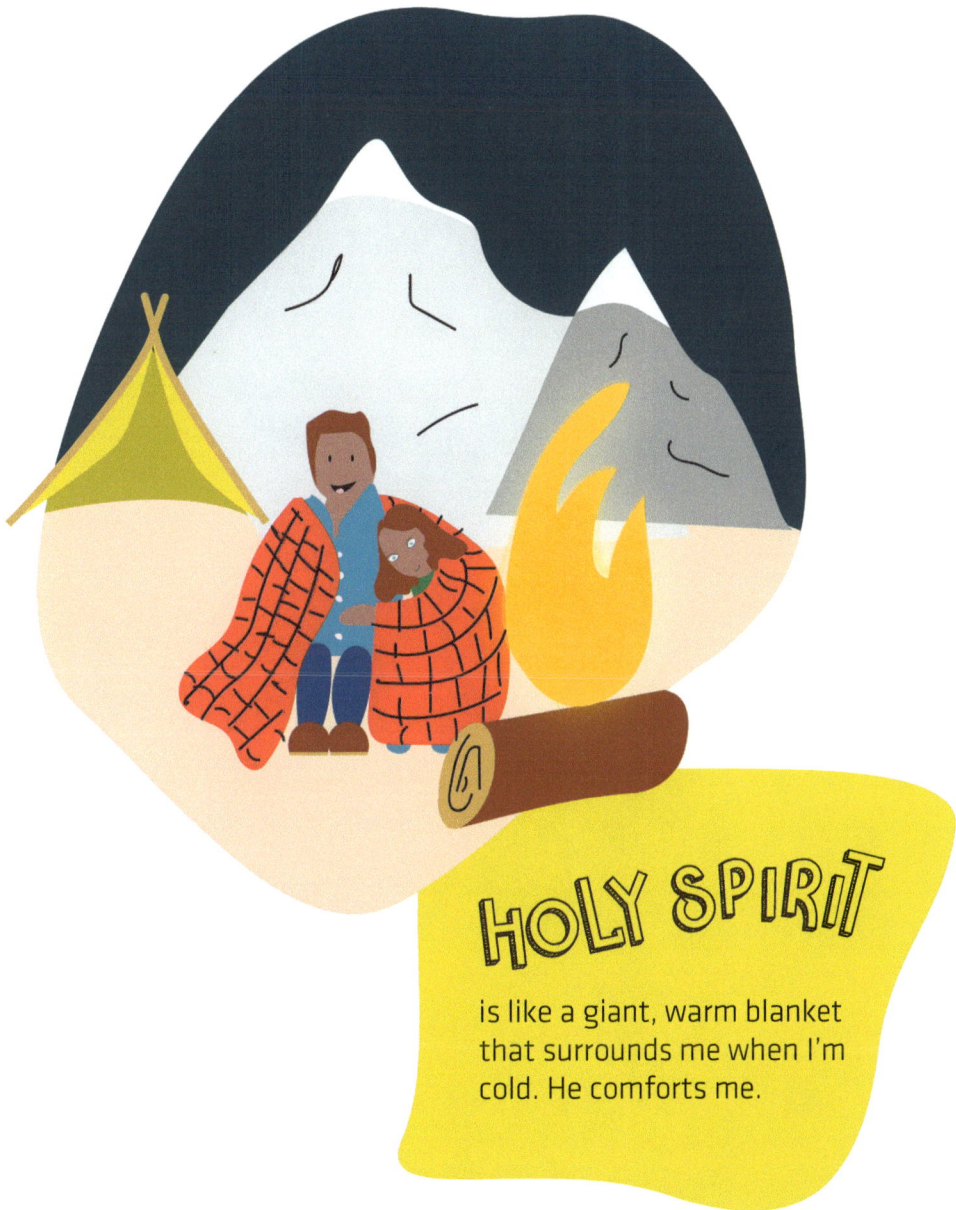

HOLY SPIRIT

is like a giant, warm blanket that surrounds me when I'm cold. He comforts me.

HOLY SPIRIT

is like a handwritten letter carefully sealed in an envelope. He is kept inside of us.

HOLY SPIRIT

is like changing from dirty play clothes into fresh clean clothes. He transforms us and cleans us up.

HOLY SPIRIT

is like a police officer directing traffic. He gives me
wisdom on the safest path. He helps me walk in the
right direction.

HOLY SPIRIT

is like riding a bike without training wheels. He helps me to do all things by His power.

HOLY SPIRIT

is like my favorite worship song. He empowers my voice to sing a new song and be refreshed in it.

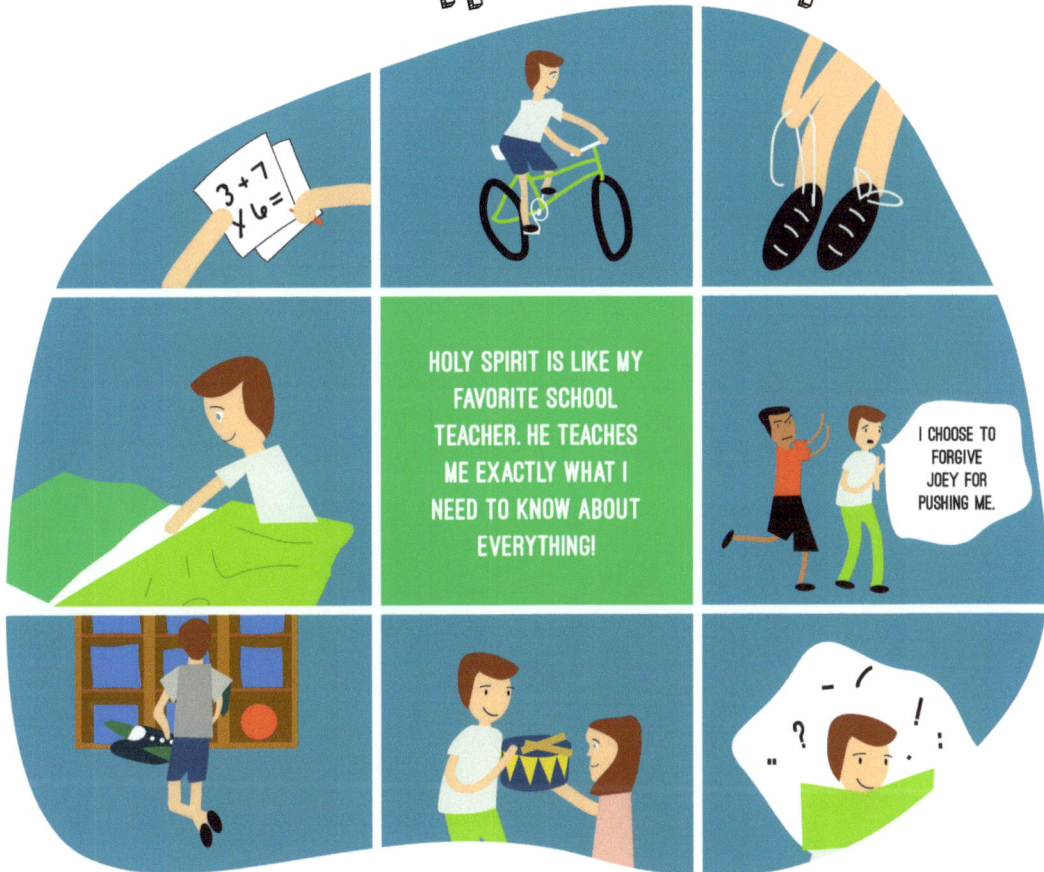

HOLY SPIRIT

HOLY SPIRIT IS LIKE MY FAVORITE SCHOOL TEACHER. HE TEACHES ME EXACTLY WHAT I NEED TO KNOW ABOUT EVERYTHING!

I CHOOSE TO FORGIVE JOEY FOR PUSHING ME.

HOLY SPIRIT

is like sharing snacks with a friend who doesn't have any. He teaches me to be kind and loving to all people.

HOLY SPIRIT

is like a cool drink of water. He fills and refreshes me when I feel hot, thirsty and dry.

PURE WATER

HOLY SPIRIT

is like a trusty side-kick puppy. He's my most loyal friend throughout the night and there with me when I wake up daily.

HOLY SPIRIT

is like jumping off the high dive at the pool. It is His strength and power that gives me the courage it takes to jump.

HOLY SPIRIT

is like reading a book without any pictures.
He helps me use my imagination.

HOLY SPIRIT

is like the game of hide and seek.
When we seek Him, He comes and
finds us with His answers.

HOLY SPIRIT

is like riding a rocket ship to outer space. He takes me to places I have never been by His Spirit.

HOLY SPIRIT

is like having dreams. He takes me to beautiful places in the heavens that we don't yet have here on Earth.

HOLY SPIRIT

is like reading directions on
how to build a city with blocks.
He gives me advice on how to
build each part.

HOLY SPIRIT

is like cleaning my room. He leads me to put everything I have in its place.

HOLY SPIRIT

is like a worship service.
Everyone in the room has their heart
focused on the Lord.

HOLY SPIRIT

is like being obedient to your mommy and daddy when they ask you to do something. I honor Him when I obey His voice.

HOLY SPIRIT

is like cleaning out my locker on the last day of school. He helps me get rid of things I don't need.

HOLY SPIRIT

is like choosing a new toy at the store. He makes me feel loved, chosen, and brings me home into His family.

HOLY SPIRIT

is like hitting a home-run at every baseball game. He coaches me through to victory when I choose to play on His team.

HOLY SPIRIT

is like a flashlight. He floods our paths with light.

HOLY SPIRIT

is like a warm bubble bath. He washes over every place in me that needs to be cleaned up.

HOLY SPIRIT

is like sitting in Mommy's lap when it's time to settle down. He brings a peace and stillness that lets me know I am safe.

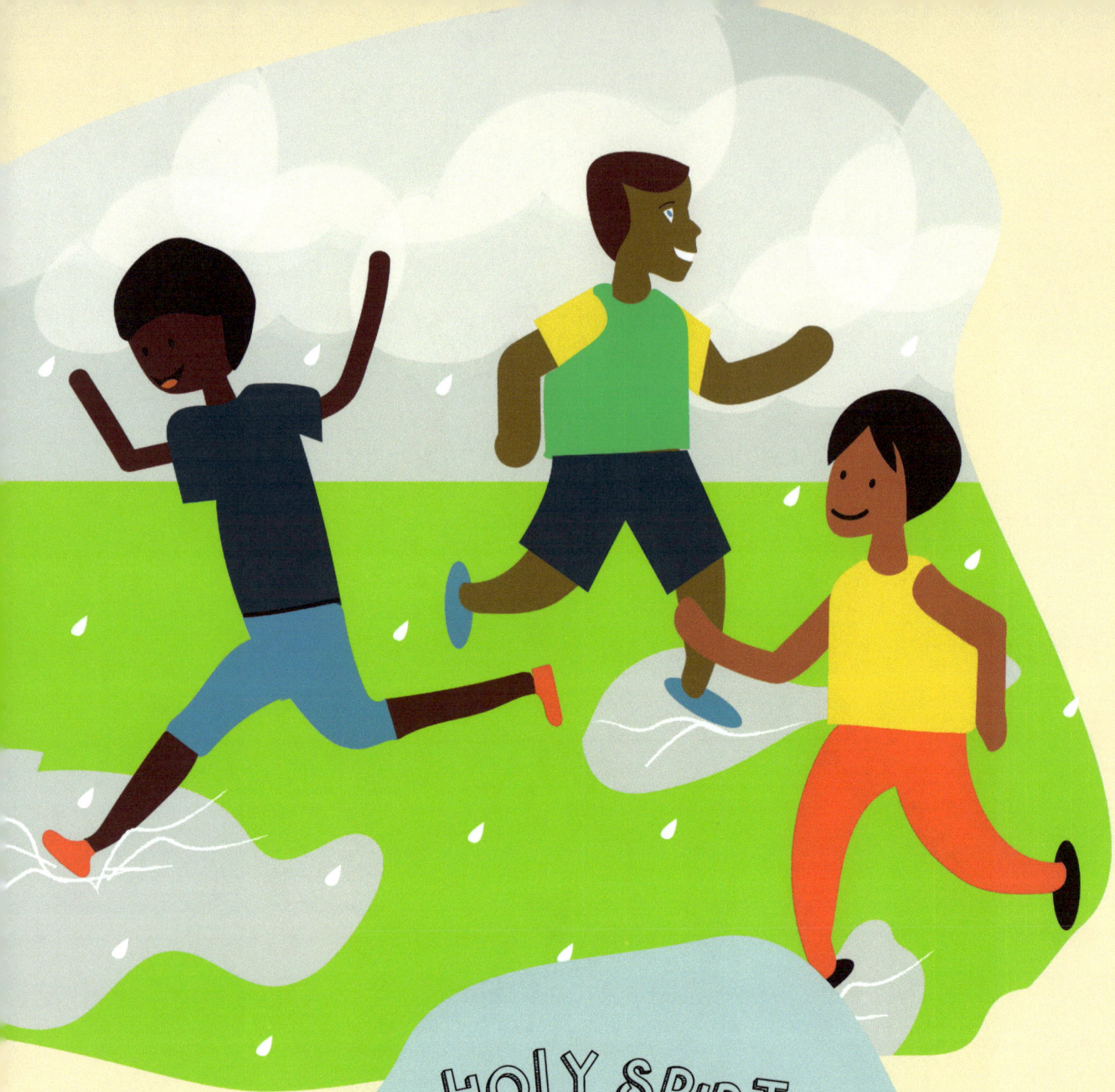

HOLY SPIRIT

is like dancing in the rain.
I am soaked in His presence
when I choose to be with Him.

HOLY SPIRIT

is like taking the lid off my cup so I can take a big drink of water. I am free to drink of Him without difficulty.

HOLY SPIRIT is like playing a game of basketball. He gives each person on the team a position to play.

HOLY SPIRIT

is like making s'mores at a campout. His fire melts and shapes me into His perfect image just like the marshmallow.

Jealous

HOLY SPIRIT

is like a teacher ringing a bell to get the classroom's attention. He wants us to look at Him. He desires to have our love and time.

www.ingramcontent.com/pod-product-compliance
Lightning Source LLC
Chambersburg PA
CBHW042014090426
42811CB00015B/1642

9 781735 546407